WHEN
PLAN B
FAILS

WHEN PLAN B FAILS

It's about how you Think...
Plan...Respond...

MARK WIENER

CONTENTS

INTRODUCTION

A Journey Through Crisis and Preparedness

We are guaranteed nothing in the current business environment. Every plan and strategy we develop is vulnerable to forces beyond our control, from technological failures to natural disasters, employee mistakes to bad actors and leadership shake-ups.

We plan for growth. We plan for success.

Too often, we *fail* to plan for disruption—especially the kind that can bring an entire company to its knees overnight.

We need to talk about what happens when Plan B fails.

I've spent years helping companies navigate crises they never saw coming. As the CEO of BizCom Global, I've seen firsthand how organizations of all sizes face catastrophic situations that could have been prevented, or at least substantially minimized. Whether it's a cyberattack, a natural disaster, or an unexpected leadership vacuum, the difference between survival and collapse often comes down to one thing: **preparedness**.

Lessons from the Front Lines

I saw firsthand what happens when decision-makers freeze in the face of an emergency.

I used to serve as a young Chief of Operations for a volunteer ambulance corps in New York City. One night, we responded to a mass-casualty incident involving six cars and a truck. More than 20 people were injured, six were critically wounded, and one person had already lost their life by the time we arrived. The scene was chaotic, filled with flashing lights, panicked bystanders, and a desperate need for order.

In moments like this, every second counts. EMTs rushed to the first victims they saw, but with limited resources, someone had to step back and see the big picture.

I was forced to make split-second decisions: how to secure the scene from further danger; where to direct immediate care; and how to allocate our finite resources to save as many lives as possible. I couldn't focus on any one crisis; tunnel vision would have led to more casualties.

That night, I learned a lesson that would shape my entire career:

A plan is useless if you don't know how to adapt it when everything falls apart.

Why Storytelling?

I believe stories make lessons stick. This book takes you on a journey through real-world scenarios, potential catastrophic situations that show how a leader's decisions shape outcomes. Through these pages, you will experience what it feels like to be:

- A business owner watching a cyberattack unfold in real time, locking down every digital asset they own.
- An executive realizing, too late, that their company's critical data backups were never tested, making recovery impossible.
- A manufacturer unable to ship orders because an IT security failure wiped out their entire operational database.

Each chapter tells a different real-world-inspired story, not to dwell on disaster, but to show how these situations could have been avoided. Some companies recovered, albeit painfully, while others never reopened.

The Common Thread: A Lack of Planning

A company's ability to survive disruption doesn't come down to luck. It depends on deliberate preparation.

Too often, organizations suffer not from a lack of intelligence or resources, but because no one stopped to ask, "*What if?*"

Take a mid-sized accounting firm I worked with, for example. They had cyber insurance, so they assumed they were protected. But they never reviewed the policy requirements.

When ransomware hit, they lost access to all client data. Their claim was denied because they didn't have multi-factor authentication or backups in place. Within 90 days, they shut their doors.

When they came to us, it was too late; the damage had already been done.

The lesson? Insurance and tools mean nothing if they're not tested and maintained.

Throughout this book, you'll see what happens when businesses fail to prepare—and what success looks like when they do. You'll learn how to assess risk, test assumptions, and make decisions that improve continuity and control.

A Personal Commitment to Resilience

As a business leader, I don't just preach preparedness. I live it.

I've dealt with technology failures, natural disasters, and leadership disruptions. Each challenge reinforced this truth:

You can't avoid every crisis, but you can be ready to respond.

Whether you're a CEO, COO, CFO, or a leader in Legal, HR, IT, or Communications—or the owner of the business—you will face a crisis. This book is designed to help you think ahead; understand your risk as it addresses people, process and technology; prepare accordingly; and avoid the mistakes that have cost others piles of money—or their entire business.

Because when disaster strikes, you won't have time to make a plan. You'll only have time to execute one.

Let's make sure you have the *right* one.

Surviving in business isn't about predicting every pitfall. It's about preparing for the unexpected and knowing how to pivot when everything falls apart.

~Mark

CHAPTER 1

The Circuit of Planning

"Everyone has a plan until they get punched in the mouth."
— Mike Tyson

Every well-crafted plan, no matter how meticulous, is only as strong as its ability to adapt when the unexpected strikes. In business—and in life—our initial blueprint is only one piece of a larger, ever-evolving circuit. This is the heart of the philosophy behind *When Plan B Fails*: planning is crucial.

It's not just about having a Plan B. It's about anticipating every twist and turn and even preparing a backup for your backup plan.

Let me tell you about a time when a lack of planning nearly led to a crisis.

The Unexpected Turn in Dallas

It was July 19 in Dallas, Texas, a day that had begun with promise at an IT conference filled with innovation. As the event wrapped up, I was set for a routine journey home on Delta Airlines: a flight from Dallas/Fort Worth (DFW) to Raleigh (RDU) with a brief connection in Atlanta (ATL). Everything seemed to be in order.

However, as I approached the gate, the atmosphere shifted dramatically. Severe weather on the East Coast had already set the stage for delays. The short layover in Atlanta was suddenly a precarious gamble against nature. In an attempt to get home on time, I allowed Delta to reroute me to Salt Lake City (SLC).

Crisis Unfolds

Then came the unexpected twist that would mark this journey as a memorable lesson.

While waiting, the digital displays around the terminal began to malfunction. One by one, the normally vibrant screens turned an eerie blue, with some even flashing the infamous blue screen of death. Amid the confusion, it became clear that something far more complex was at play than just weather delays.

News reports soon confirmed the scale of the disruption. The culprit? A system-wide IT failure, later traced publicly to an issue involving CrowdStrike, a well-known cybersecurity firm.

Delta's internal systems, crucial for weight balancing and flight coordination, were down, throwing a wrench into their most basic functions of air travel. Their fleet had to halt operations immediately.

Other carriers, like Sun Country Air, managed to keep their operations moving. Their ground staff went back to basics. Staff filled out boarding passes by hand. They used offline spreadsheets to calculate weight balances. It wasn't glamorous, but it worked.

The contrast was striking. Their resourcefulness underscored a vital lesson:

Sometimes, resilience isn't about technological sophistication, but about fallback options.

A Day of Trials and Unexpected Adventures

Despite the chaos, at 11:30 PM, we finally boarded the Delta flight.

Unfortunately, the troubles were far from over. The crew's attempts at weight balancing were futile without access to their automated systems. What was initially posed as a short delay stretched into a 45-minute ordeal, after which we were forced to disembark. It soon became evident, from both the disjointed airport operations and the emerging news stories, that the IT failure was more extensive than anyone had anticipated.

Stranded in an airport that felt like a modern-day purgatory, I ended up spending the night amid a surreal series of airport adventures. Conversations with fellow passengers revealed a shared sentiment of disbelief. The incident, now clearly attributed to the cascading fallout from the CrowdStrike-related system glitch, was a stark reminder of the fragility inherent in even the most sophisticated plans.

The next day brought further twists. I was rerouted to Austin, Texas, on a flight destined for Raleigh. Yet, fate was not done testing our resilience. A two-hour delay to Austin meant that the connecting flight to Raleigh departed without me. In a final twist of serendipity, Delta scrambled to add an extra flight to accommodate stranded passengers. While enroute to Austin again, I luckily managed to secure one of the few remaining seats on the additional flight.

In the end, my journey that day—from a routine flight to an unexpected odyssey—became a vivid illustration of why planning is crucial. It's not about avoiding every disruption, but about designing systems robust enough to pivot when those disruptions inevitably occur.

Welcome to *When Plan B Fails*, where every setback is an opportunity to learn, adapt, and build a more resilient future.

That day illustrated why "What if?" planning is instrumental in business operations. You don't just need one contingency—you need several that are layered and tested.

Lessons Learned: Adaptability

- **Expect the Unpredictable:** Even a perfect plan can collapse under the weight of real-world disruptions such as weather, technology, or people.

- **Embrace Layered Contingencies:** The best resilience strategies include backups for your backups, which may include manual workarounds.

- **Value Adaptability Over Perfection:** In both travel and business, the ability to pivot and improvise in the face of chaos is far more valuable than a rigid, flawless plan.

Key Takeaways for Executives

- Conduct regular stress tests across departments and systems to identify vulnerabilities in your operational plans
- Build contingency plans with depth for critical processes, and not just failovers, but full manual workarounds.
- Train teams for real-world crisis scenarios and empower decision-making.
- Monitor and diversify technology dependencies.
- Debrief after every disruption to refine future responses.

Final Thoughts: Plan B Isn't Enough

Backup plans are only as good as their adaptability.

As this chapter demonstrates, it's rarely one single event that causes a breakdown. It's the chain reaction that follows when plans don't evolve fast enough.

For executives, business leaders, and decision-makers, the key takeaway is this: **resilience isn't about preventing every crisis, but about having the flexibility, resources, and mindset to**

respond effectively when things go wrong. Whether in travel, operations, or business continuity planning, the ability to pivot under pressure can mean the difference between disruption and disaster.

In the chapters ahead, we'll explore scenarios where assumptions, inaction and poor communication triggered far worse outcomes than the original crisis. Each story will underline the same truth:

Real resilience is built by leaders who anticipate, adapt, and act before everything is on the line.

"It is not the strongest of the species that survive, nor the most intelligent, but the one most responsive to change."

—Charles Darwin

CHAPTER 2

The Domino Effect—When Disruption Hits Home

"For the want of a nail, the shoe was lost.
"For the want of a shoe, the horse was lost.
"For the want of a horse, the rider was lost.
"For the want of a rider, the battle was lost.
"For the want of a battle, the kingdom was lost.
"And all for the want of a horseshoe nail."

—Ancient Proverb

In business, disruptions rarely arrive with sirens or headlines. They sneak in quietly, sometimes disguised as delays or minor miscommunications, until they cascade into full-blown crises. As we explored in Chapter 1, layered contingency planning is vital. Now, we delve into a real-world scenario where multiple unforeseen events tested the resilience of Vertex Trucks, a mid-sized manufacturer of specialty vehicles.

The Calm Before the Storm

Vertex Trucks was thriving. Known for their rugged, specialty trucks, they had built a strong reputation for producing high-quality, customizable trucks in a competitive market.

The operation was lean but mature. Their supply chain was a careful balancing act: multiple vendors supported key parts, inventory stayed light to reduce overhead, and their just-in-time delivery model was coordinated through a mix of routine logistics and automated tracking systems.

On paper, the supply chain was robust, perhaps even enviable for a mid-sized manufacturer. But it masked a deeper vulnerability that wasn't fully understood until it was too late.

At the heart of the issue was Vertex's dependence on hundreds of aging microchips embedded in the truck chassis control systems. These low-cost components, though unassuming and widely available pre-pandemic, were essential to the entire product. It was a design legacy common across the commercial trucking industry. And in Vertex's case, it was about to become the bottleneck that brought everything else to a stop.

The Fire That Lit the Fuse

Early in 2020, Vertex's world changed overnight. A fire broke out in their paint plant, the final step in their production process. Several dozen nearly complete trucks were destroyed. The facility itself was left unusable. The fire dominated local news cycles. Footage of smoking steel and charred frames was shared across social media.

But behind the scenes, the problems ran deeper. Production came to a hard stop. Orders were delayed indefinitely. Assembly schedules collapsed.

The paint plant fire was bad, but it was about to get worse. Within weeks, the COVID-19 pandemic began disrupting global logistics. Factory shutdowns, raw material shortages, and international shipping delays made everything more difficult.

For Vertex, the most urgent issue became sourcing new chassis. Every one of their chassis vendors reported upstream problems. Delays lengthened. Contracts slipped. And then came the realization: it wasn't the chassis vendors themselves that were failing—it was the semiconductor manufacturers they relied on.

The Microchip Shortage

As global demand for personal electronics, medical devices, and remote work tools exploded, chip manufacturers made a logical business decision: pivot toward higher-margin components. The result was a massive contraction in the availability of legacy microchips, precisely the type used in Vertex's trucks. These chips didn't offer high profits, and demand had been shrinking for years—until it wasn't.

Even though Vertex's chassis suppliers remained technically operational, their manufacturing capacity had been gutted by a lack of semiconductors. When shipments weren't canceled outright, the chassis that did arrive were often missing critical components.

This wasn't just a supply issue. It was a design risk disguised as an inventory problem.

Across the broader automotive industry, similar stories played out. Major brands halted production. Some turned to redesigning vehicles with alternate chips. Others began stockpiling what they could. Vertex, with fewer resources and smaller contracts, had no leverage. And their challenges weren't just external.

When It Rains, It Pours

By mid-2021, Vertex had barely started to recover from the fire and supply chain shock when another blow landed. A powerful tornado tore through the region, ripping the roof off one of their primary assembly lines. The storm caused millions of structural damage, but more pressingly, it rendered an entire lot of 23 units in the manufacturing process unusable.

The company's financial foundation was now at risk. They pursued bank loans and bridge financing just to maintain operations. Management was spending time working on the grants and loans and dealing with broader financial issues. Overtime was eliminated, production hours were scaled back, and timelines were missed. Customers, some of whom had been with Vertex for over a decade, began demanding assurances the company couldn't give them.

Engineering was working overtime to redesign certain elements using alternate components. But even those efforts were delayed. New engineers had been hired, but their workstations were on backorder for months. Nothing was moving fast enough.

Internally, Vertex's small IT team was overwhelmed. Their systems were designed for efficiency, not agility. Now, they were patching together vendor portals, modifying workflows, and handling a flood of user issues, all while reconfiguring backend systems that hadn't been touched in years. Reports didn't match inventory. Routing conflicts caused duplicate orders. And without proper integration support, visibility vanished.

The Breakdown of Plan B

Vertex had always touted its contingency plan. There were alternate vendors, documented emergency protocols, and modest reserves of key materials.But no part of the plan accounted for what happened: simultaneous, compounding events that triggered failure across multiple domains.

- The fire disrupted operations and deliveries.
- COVID broke the global supply chain.
- The tornado wrecked facilities.
- The semiconductor shortage made alternate parts impossible to procure.
- The engineering team was immobilized.
- IT systems buckled.
- And the leadership team was too thin to manage all fronts at once—vendor relations, insurance negotiations, disaster recovery, and customer management.

Lessons Learned: When Resilience Gets Real

- One crisis tests operations. Multiple crises test leadership, communication, and culture.
- True IT resilience means systems can adapt—not just recover—from unexpected changes.
- Supplier diversity is meaningless without supplier priority. Contracts and relationships matter.

Key Takeaways for Executives

- Don't just plan for a failure—plan for three failures at once. That's when systems are truly exposed.
- Evaluate your IT systems not for uptime, but for visibility, flexibility, and manual override capacity.
- Treat every critical supplier as a partner. Review how you rank with them during global shortages.

Final Thoughts: A Wounded Company That Endured

In spite of their hardships, Vertex didn't collapse.

They stabilized operations and rebuilt the damaged plant. Most of their core team stayed. But the cost was real: key customers left, growth targets were missed, and product development was put on hold.

In the years since, they've invested in resilience. Contracts now include surge-priority clauses. Their IT team has grown, and infrastructure has been redesigned to support real-time updates.

They now perform quarterly continuity drills that include simulated supply and infrastructure failure.

But the path to get there was painful.

In business, it's rarely the first problem that does the damage. It's the cascade—the chain reaction of overlooked dependencies, incomplete plans, and underfunded infrastructure. What Vertex faced was a perfect storm, but their response became a case study in how to transform pain into capability.

To help other companies avoid similar blind spots, BizCom Global now offers hands-on Incident Response Experiences. These are scenario-based programs for leadership teams to train for moments when things go sideways. While the simulated crises often begin in IT or cybersecurity, the lessons apply across the entire business—impacting supply chain, operations, and beyond. See the resources section for more information on how to schedule a session for your organization.

"It takes 20 years to build a reputation and five minutes to ruin it. If you think about that, you'll do things differently."
—Warren Buffett

CHAPTER 3

Drenched by Disaster—When the Floodgates Open

"It wasn't raining when Noah built the ark."

—Howard Ruff

When Hurricane Beryl made landfall in Houston, few could predict the chain reaction it would set in motion.

It wasn't just neighborhoods and infrastructure that bore the brunt of the storm. Businesses, many of which had weathered smaller disruptions for years, were caught unprepared. For Lone Star Claims Adjusters, a mid-sized insurance adjustment firm rooted in Houston, the storm exposed vulnerabilities that had long gone unnoticed. What followed was not only a crisis of infrastructure, but also of leadership, technology, and continuity planning.

Trusted by Many, Unprepared for One

Lone Star had spent nearly two decades building its reputation. With a team of seasoned claims adjusters, they were known for delivering fast, accurate evaluations to insurance carriers across Texas. The firm operated primarily from a downtown Houston office, housing its full staff and all operational infrastructure under one roof. Despite the evolution of remote work and cloud technology, Lone Star had taken a conservative approach, preferring localized control over digital flexibility.

Their primary claims system was installed on a local server maintained in-house. A handful of documents had migrated to a cloud platform, but critical tools, including customer files, adjuster notes, and communications logs, remained grounded in the office. Only two employees were set up for remote access, and even then, the scope was limited to administrative tasks.

The Waterline Moment

When the levees failed and floodwaters began to rise, it didn't take long for chaos to reach Lone Star's doorstep. Within hours, the office was inaccessible. By the next morning, water had filled the first floor and continued climbing. Desks were submerged. Computers, servers, paper files—everything essential to their business was submerged and either destroyed or swept away.

Due to the storm, they became the victim that normally needed their services. The outage was complete: Phone lines were dead, email servers were unresponsive, and claims adjusters were locked out of the systems they needed for client communications and assessment filing. With no working disaster recovery plan in place, leadership had no immediate answers for employees, clients, or partners.

Scrambling to Stay Afloat

What followed in the days after the flood was a patchwork of improvised fixes. Leadership held emergency meetings from personal cell phones. Adjusters used their own laptops to communicate with clients, but without access to core systems, their hands were tied.

The two remote-enabled employees tried to establish some form of triage, but their reach was limited. There were no pre-established protocols for rerouting communication or activating a decentralized command structure.

Employees drove to nearby cities to find dry office space. Temporary servers were rented. But even with these efforts, the damage had already been done. Claims went unanswered. Timelines slipped. And clients, many of whom were experiencing flood damage of their own, were left in limbo.

The Clients Who Couldn't Wait

Within a week, several of Lone Star's key insurance carrier partners began raising concerns. Missed deadlines, unclear updates, and silence from leadership created a credibility vacuum.

What began as inquiries quickly turned into ultimatums. Three long-time insurance clients pulled their contracts and moved to competitors who had better resilience in place. The loss of trust was as damaging as the flood itself.

Lone Star's failure didn't stem from a lack of effort; the team was dedicated. Staff were willing to work long hours and make personal sacrifices to restore service. But intention couldn't make up for missing systems, untested backups, and the lack of a structured response plan.

The Technology that Couldn't Swim

The company's IT infrastructure had always been viewed as a cost center, something to maintain but not to evolve. Over the years, proposals to shift core applications to the cloud or build out a virtual desktop infrastructure were dismissed as unnecessary expenses. Now, those decisions had a price.

Recovery efforts were slow. Immediate restoration from backups was impossible because physical drives had been destroyed. Attempts to pull data from offsite archives were hampered by outdated formats and a lack of documentation. Even simple processes, like resetting passwords or provisioning new devices, were slowed by the absence of a central control system.

By the time core systems were operational again, nearly three weeks later, the business had already lost ground it couldn't reclaim. Former clients weren't interested in explanations. They had already moved on.

Lessons Learned: Resilience Isn't Built in the Rain

- You can't delegate continuity planning; executives must own it.
- Physical backups are only as useful as the environment protecting them.
- Remote access is no longer optional, it's foundational.
- Technology is not just a tool, it's a strategy.
- Every employee must know their role when the plan is activated.

Key Takeaways for Executives

- Move core operations into cloud-based platforms with geographic redundancy.
- Conduct annual disaster simulations (at a minimum) that include full system shutdowns.
- Develop a tiered crisis communication plan and test it semi-annually.
- Invest in mobile-friendly workstations and enforce offsite access protocols.
- Reframe IT as a strategic function, not just a support service.

Final Thoughts: After the Storm

Lone Star Claims Adjusters didn't fail from a lack of hard work. They failed from a lack of foresight.

They were the kind of company that had survived plenty of small storms, but they weren't prepared for a perfect one. By the time the skies cleared, their most valuable asset, trust, had been washed away. Companies that rely on short-term success without establishing strong contingency plans leave themselves vulnerable to catastrophic failure.

For leaders, the key takeaway is simple: **Business continuity planning is not a checkbox. It is a full contact sport that requires leadership, foresight, and continuous engagement**. Every organization, no matter the size, must build resilience through proactive planning, redundancy measures, and crisis simulations.

As you think about your own organization, ask this: are you planning for the crisis you've already seen, or the one that hasn't arrived yet? Because the next storm is coming. The only question is whether your business is ready to weather it.

"By failing to prepare, you are preparing to fail."
—Benjamin Franklin

CHAPTER 4

The Cost of Cutting Corners

"If you think technology can solve your security problems, then you don't understand the problems—and you don't understand the technology."

—Bruce Schneier

In manufacturing, decisions are often driven by efficiency. Every executive knows that margins matter and that every dollar saved is a dollar earned. Sometimes, the desire to trim costs in the short term leads to devastating consequences down the road.

This is the story of cost control and lean operations. While these strategies can lead to profit and scalability, they can also create blind spots.

This was the reality at Northpoint Precision Manufacturing, which was known for its commitment to quality, efficiency and reliability.

When a cyberattack struck, the absence of modern IT infrastructure, tools, controls, and processes left their business exposed. The attack nearly brought the company to its knees. And the root cause wasn't just how the bad actors got in—it was a culture that viewed technology as a cost center rather than a strategic investment. What unfolded offers a sobering reminder: cutting corners in cybersecurity can cost far more than any short-term savings.

A Foundation Built on Assumptions

Northpoint was respected in its sector. With over 200 employees and multiple production lines, the company provided high-precision components to clients across several industries.

Beneath this strong external brand was an overstretched IT department of just four people. Their responsibilities spanned from network and server security to machine software updates, ERP and CRM support, without any external support.

Two years before the crisis, the company initiated a major infrastructure upgrade. The IT manager recommended bringing in third-party specialists to review configurations and validate security. Leadership declined the proposal.

"We've got smart people in-house," one executive said. "We'll figure it out."

That decision would later prove costly.

Red Flags in the Rearview

A few months after the upgrade, external auditors flagged critical risks. Software patches were months behind, exposing systems to common vulnerabilities (CVEs). Default administrative credentials were still in place. Even worse, backups weren't encrypted or routinely tested.

When the findings were presented, IT was directed to "prioritize the most important issues." But without additional resources or the authority to enforce changes, little progress was made. Most vulnerabilities lingered: undocumented, untracked, and unresolved.

Leadership remained focused on product delivery, expansion, and lean budgeting. Cybersecurity felt like a theoretical risk— important in principle, but never urgent in practice. The assumption was that if nothing had happened yet, the systems must be fine.

The Breach That Changed Everything

On a Monday morning in March, Northpoint's team came in expecting business as usual.

What they found instead were frozen screens, inaccessible files, and a ransom note.

They were breached. Hackers had infiltrated the system, encrypted the company's data, and deleted backups. Operations stopped immediately and their production lines which relied on these systems were debilitated.

Every aspect of production was impacted due to the compromised systems. From part specs to client orders, nothing could move forward. Even basic business operation functions like accounting, invoicing, and payroll were offline. The internal IT team worked around the clock alongside an external incident response team referred by their cyber liability insurer. With no clean backup to restore from, the company recovery was significantly hampered.

More than 25,000 employee work hours were lost before production partially resumed. It required heavy manual intervention, as systems continued to be recovered and rebuilt from scratch.

Leadership made the strategic decision not to pay the ransom. It was the right call ethically. Operationally, recovering without a base to start from was incredibly difficult. Fortunately, one 6-month-outdated offline backup had been sent to a vendor during a planned system migration (that never occurred). That backup became the foundation. Teams used email records, printed ship records, and inventory documents to recreate thousands of transactions across sales, accounting, inventory, and shipping.

Damage Beyond Dollars

The attack made headlines in industry circles. Clients began calling, asking for delivery updates and assurances, most of which couldn't be provided. Some paused contracts until they better understood the scope of the breach. Others feared their own data had been compromised. Many quietly migrated to competitors.

This wasn't just a technical failure. It became a reputational crisis

Northpoint's leadership scrambled to retain confidence. Consultants were brought in. New firewalls were deployed. Secure access protocols were rushed into place. But the momentum was already lost—nearly six weeks passed before the company could fulfill its first post-breach order. The backlog would take another three months, with many hours of overtime, to clear.

When the dust settled, it was clear that Northpoint was underinsured and unprepared financially. The total cost, including direct losses, emergency consulting, delayed revenue, and churned clients, was over three million dollars. That figure didn't include opportunity cost, lost trust, employee wages lost during downtime, or the strain on leadership and staff.

Their cyber liability insurance paid about $750,000. They were lucky to have the resources to recover at all.

The Road Back to Resilience

In the aftermath, Northpoint rebuilt not just their systems, but their mindset.

They contracted BizCom Global to provide advisory, monitoring, and management services alongside their internal team. A multi-year digital resilience plan was drafted, funded, and implemented. Semi-annual tabletop exercises became the norm. Every new project now included a business risk and security assessment.

With guidance from BizCom's team, executives began to discuss risk tolerance and risk exposure. IT became a strategic partner, no longer just an internal service provider. Most importantly, the lessons weren't just captured in reports. They were operationalized and lived every day.

Lessons Learned: Cost Cuts Can Cut Deep

- Northpoint's story is one of avoidable loss, a reactive financial strategy, and leadership under pressure. They had every opportunity to strengthen their defenses, yet they chose to push back against the very measures that would have protected them.
- IT must be represented at the leadership level to influence strategy.
- Backups must be **encrypted, tested, and segregated** (ideally immutable).
- Security audits are only useful if acted upon.
- Culture drives continuity. When security is optional, failure is inevitable.
- Every crisis is a test of leadership. Clarity, decisiveness, speed and accountability matter.

Key Takeaways for Executives

- Cyber insurance is not a substitute for preparation.
- Make sure your insured limits account for your risk.
- Budget for IT risk assessments and disaster recovery simulations.
- Recognize that IT doesn't just support the business, but enables it.

Final Thoughts: Invest Upfront or Pay Later

Northpoint survived. But they learned the hard way that survival isn't the same as success. They spent thousands of hours rebuilding systems, regaining client trust, and restoring team morale.

In hindsight, the cost of preparedness would have been a fraction of the cost of recovery.

Your business might never face the same breach. Yet no organization is immune from disruption. The question is whether it will happen on your terms or someone else's. Resilience is built now, not in the aftermath.

When Plan B fails, the cost of avoidance will always exceed the cost of preparation.

"An ounce of prevention is worth a pound of cure."
—Benjamin Franklin

CHAPTER 5

Risk Assessments Aren't Optional

"Risk comes from not knowing what you're doing."
—Warren Buffett

There's a dangerous moment in every business lifecycle. It doesn't show up on a balance sheet or reveal itself during a product launch. It creeps in slowly, right after things start going well, while sales are growing, teams are humming, and processes feel dialed in.

What you can't see is what can hurt you most. And that's why the most successful businesses today are turning to something deceptively simple, but strategically powerful: a technology and business risk assessment.

Let me tell you about a firm that didn't see the impending disaster—and didn't listen when they were warned.

The Firm That Said No

A while back, I met with the managing partner of an accounting firm. They were trying to grow fast, expanding into several new markets and taking on bigger, more regulated clients. We offered them our 5 Pillar Business & Technology Risk Assessment—a simple way to gain visibility into their operational, cybersecurity, and compliance risks.

They declined. "Our IT guy handles all that, and besides, we also already have an MSP," the partner told us. "We are mostly cloud-based anyway. We're good."

They weren't.

A few months later, the firm was hit with a Business Email Compromise (BEC) attack. This wasn't your standard invoice fraud. The attackers used compromised credentials to impersonate internal staff, then leveraged that access to infiltrate client environments.

At the time, the firm was managing sensitive merger due diligence. Using a senior specialist's email account, the attackers sent phishing emails disguised as legitimate updates. Two clients clicked. Both suffered ransomware infections.

The fallout was brutal:

- Lawsuits from clients alleging negligence.
- A key corporate account terminated the relationship.

- Regulatory subpoenas for potential third-party breach exposure.
- Insurance complications due to missing multi-factor authentication and inadequate user training.

When I reached out, the managing partner admitted, "We probably should've done the assessment. We just didn't think something like this could happen to us."

Yet, they still declined to work with us.

"We've got it under control," he said.

I'm still not sure what that meant. We haven't heard from them since.

The 5 Pillars Assessment could have identified many of the issues.

The **BizCom Global 5 Pillar Business and Technology Assessment** offers a structured view of your organization's technology, security, continuity, and compliance maturity. It's a strategic lens on real-world risk.

We evaluate each business through five key lenses:

1. **Cybersecurity:** Are your systems secured, monitored, and hardened against threats like ransomware?

2. **Managed IT:** Are systems current, users trained, and processes mapped to avoid bottlenecks and single points of failure?

3. **IT Ecosystem:** Are your platforms and tools helping— or creating risk through fragmentation or obsolescence?

4. **Compliance:** Are you meeting the spirit and letter of your regulatory, contractual, or industry standards?

5. **Business Continuity:** If systems fail, can you recover? Are your plans documented, funded, and understood?

Each pillar is viewed through **People, Process, and Technology**:

- **People**: Are responsibilities clear? Is the team trained and ready?

- **Process**: Are workflows documented or reliant on tribal knowledge?

- **Technology**: Are tools secure and scalable, or stitched together ad hoc?

The result is a clear, actionable snapshot:

- Where you stand today?
- Where your real risks and inefficiencies lie?
- What a smarter, more resilient version of your operation looks like?

No bloated reports. Just clarity, direction, and next steps.

More than a Risk Report: A Map for the Future

The assessment isn't just about avoiding disasters. It helps executive teams make smarter decisions aligned with growth and risk tolerance.

You can use it to:

- Justify hiring a compliance lead.
- Map the cost of shadow IT.
- Prepare strategy to be able to get cyber insurance discounts.
- Guide vendor or infrastructure decisions.

It's a filter for smarter strategy.

Before the Next Curve

In Chapter 3, we saw a claims company lose business because they couldn't access systems after a flood.

In Chapter 4, a manufacturer's breach revealed years of ignored gaps—and cost them their competitive edge.

Each could've benefited from knowing their risks sooner.

The 5 Pillar Risk Assessment delivers real insight. It's fast, collaborative, and focused—and it shifts the conversation from uncertainty to confident action.

Your Next Best Step

If you've made it this far, you already know: Plan A doesn't always work. Plan B might not either. So, what now?

The companies that grow after crisis are the ones who invest in visibility, clarity, and honest assessments before something breaks.

We designed the 5 Pillar Risk Assessment to be that first step.

No pressure. No obligation. A clear opportunity to understand your risk before it turns into impact.

"Plans are only good intentions unless they immediately degenerate into hard work."

—Peter Drucker

CHAPTER 6

Navigating the Storm— A Car Dealership's Cyberattack Ordeal

"You can't stop the waves, but you can learn to surf."
—Jon Kabat-Zinn

In the summer of 2024, the automotive industry faced an unprecedented disruption.

It didn't begin with a chip shortage, a financial crash, or a vehicle recall. It started with a software provider.

Modern car dealerships rely heavily on integrated systems for everything from inventory and CRM to service scheduling and payment processing. One of the most widely adopted platforms is CDK Global, used by thousands of dealerships across North America.

On June 19th, that system went dark.

This chapter recounts the experience of Greenfield Motors, a mid-sized dealership chain in the Southeast, as it navigated the aftermath of the CDK Global ransomware attack. It's a story not just about IT, but also resilience, customer communication, leadership under pressure, and the importance of preparing for third-party risks.

The Day the Screens Went Dark

Greenfield Motors had four locations and roughly 80 employees across its service, sales, and back-office departments. Their entire operation ran through CDK: scheduling, invoicing, parts tracking, customer communications, and payroll tracking.

On June 19, 2024, employees at Greenfield Motors arrived to find their computer systems unresponsive. The usual rhythm of activity was replaced by confusion. Attempts to access inventory, process sales, or schedule service appointments were met with blank screens and error messages. They weren't yet aware that CDK Global had suffered a crippling ransomware attack.

At first, the outage was brushed off as temporary. CDK's status page acknowledged a system-wide issue, and internal teams were told they would update shortly. Hours turned into days, and days stretched into weeks. During that time, Greenfield's staff scrambled to function without their primary systems.

Operational Chaos: From Digital to Manual

Technicians resorted to whiteboards to log appointments. Salespeople dug through printed forms they hadn't used in years. Managers scribbled VINs and service histories on sticky notes. It was a complete throwback to the pre-digital era. This wasn't sustainable!

The service department, which normally processed 80 cars a day, was suddenly limited to 30. Delays in ordering parts, obtaining warranty approvals, and closing service tickets became the new norm. Frustrated customers aired their grievances on social media, and some took their business to competing dealerships.

The general manager of Greenfield's flagship store was constantly on the phone. Some customers were patient. Others were not. Frontline employees bore the brunt of the frustration, and morale began to crack. The worst part? There was still no clear timeline for recovery.

Eventually, the team implemented a patchwork solution using spreadsheets, cloud-stored backups, and shared documents to track open issues. It was far from ideal, but it allowed the business to limp forward.

CDK's system recovery began incrementally, but full functionality would not return for weeks. To make matters worse, uncertainty about customer data exposure hovered over every conversation. CDK's initial public statements were vague. Had customer names, contact details, or financial records been compromised? No one could say. Customers began calling—not just to reschedule appointments, but to ask whether their identities were at risk.

Financial Freefall

As the outage dragged into its second week, Greenfield Motors made the difficult decision to pause new car sales. Without accurate credit checks and financing tools, each transaction carried significant risk. Payroll had to be outsourced and processed manually. Parts inventory became a guessing game, as no system reconciliations were possible.

The financial impact on Greenfield Motors was swift and painful.

- **Revenue Decline:** Vehicle sales fell sharply as processing delays caused customers to abandon deals.

- **Service Revenue:** The service department saw a downturn due to scheduling issues and extended turnaround times.

- **Cash Flow Crunch:** With income down, the dealership struggled to meet basic obligations like payroll and supplier payments.

This scenario was not unique. The Anderson Economic Group estimated that the CDK Global outage cost auto dealerships over $1 billion in direct losses. Major dealership groups cited steep earnings declines linked directly to the incident.

The Long Road Back

In the aftermath, Greenfield made significant changes. They created a third-party risk register, identifying their most critical vendors and outlining what would happen if each failed. They began duplicating customer records to an encrypted cloud backup. Fallback procedures were created for every department.

Yet, challenges remained. They were still dependent on a handful of key vendors—and had no systems in place to replace them in a true emergency. The lesson was clear: trust is not a strategy.

Greenfield began participating in industry-wide reviews of CDK's performance and started evaluating modular alternatives. Their new motto was short and clear: *"Outsource the function, not the responsibility."*

Lessons Learned: Third-Party Dependencies Are Your Risk, Too

- The CDK Global cyberattack served as a wake-up call for the dealership industry.
- A system you don't control is still your responsibility when it fails.
- Your crisis playbook must account for vendor outages, not just internal failures.
- Clear communication builds trust. Vague updates erode it.
- Manual fallback procedures, no matter how outdated, can save the day.

- The customer experience doesn't stop during disruption, it just gets harder to manage.

Key Takeaways for Executives

- Audit your vendors you rely on most, including your cloud and SaaS platforms.
- Require business continuity and incident response clauses in vendor contracts. Build manual fallback processes for essential functions like sales, payments, and scheduling.
- Train your leadership team to make decisions without technology, not just with it.

Final Thoughts: Don't Outsource Accountability

Greenfield Motors endured the CDK Global ransomware attack, but not without scars. The experience forced leadership to confront uncomfortable truths about over-reliance, vendor transparency, and preparedness.

Third-party vendors make modern business possible. However, they also create invisible dependencies. When those systems fail, the consequences are felt on your P&L, in your brand, and inside your boardroom.

Outsourcing doesn't absolve responsibility. Your business reputation and operational continuity still rest with you.

Prepare accordingly, because when Plan B fails, finger-pointing won't bring your business back online.

"Hope is not a strategy."

—Vince Lombardi

CHAPTER 7

When the Lifeline Breaks

"We are only as strong as our weakest link."

—Unknown

Healthcare and cybersecurity are now inseparable. A breach doesn't just affect data; it affects people.

Trust is Broken

In healthcare, trust is everything. Patients place their lives in the hands of their providers and medical practices. In turn, the practices rely on a complex web of systems and partners to ensure that care is delivered efficiently and billing runs smoothly.

On February 21, 2024, that trust was put to the test when Change Healthcare, a company responsible for processing nearly half of all medical claims in the United States, was crippled by a ransomware attack. Within hours, thousands of clinics lost access to critical services: claim submission, payment processing, and insurance verification.

This chapter tells the story of Riverside Family Clinic, a mid-sized primary care and pediatrics group based in the Midwest. The clinic employed 14 providers and served over 6,000 active patients annually. They were no stranger to tight margins and long days, but nothing could have prepared them for the operational standstill that followed.

The Day Everything Stopped

Riverside's entire revenue cycle management pipeline ran through Change Healthcare. When the breach hit, it was as if someone had flipped a switch. Appointment reminders failed. Insurance eligibility checks timed out. Claim submissions were rejected. Payments stopped arriving.

By the tenth day, the clinic had over 3,500 unsubmitted claims sitting in their billing queue. Cash flow slowed to a trickle. Their EHR vendor issued emergency patches for offline data entry, but without Change Healthcare's integration, they couldn't communicate with payers. Patients still needed care, but the financial engine behind the scenes was clogged.

The office manager began triaging appointments by payer. Medicaid and Medicare patients, normally deprioritized due to lower reimbursement rates, were moved to the top of the list because the clinic could still submit those claims manually. Visits from patients with commercial insurance were spaced out to conserve resources. The billing team worked long hours, trying to find alternate submission methods, often receiving conflicting information from insurance carriers.

It wasn't just Riverside. Across the country, thousands of clinics and hospitals were experiencing the same problem. For a small, independent practice like Riverside, the impact was immediate. Unlike larger health systems, they didn't have financial reserves to cover months of lost revenue.

The Ripple Effect: From Billing to Payroll to Patient Care

Desperate for a solution, the leadership team turned to their bank for a line of credit. But without a clear timeline for resuming claims processing, they couldn't provide the financial projections required to secure funding.

By the fourth week, payroll was on the line. Several front office staff were placed on temporary furlough. Overtime was eliminated. Some providers voluntarily deferred part of their salaries to keep the doors open. Morale dropped sharply.

Patients began noticing the strain. Phone wait times grew longer. Prescription delays became common. Some families began transferring their care to larger health systems that remained unaffected by the outage.

Internally, clinic leadership held tense daily meetings. Their IT provider had little visibility, since the root of the problem was upstream. Their cyber liability insurance provider advised waiting for more information before triggering breach protocols. The result was a fog of indecision—and no clear path forward.

When Change Healthcare finally acknowledged the breach and disclosed its scope, the damage had already been done. Riverside had lost more than $280,000 in delayed reimbursements within the first month. Over 10% of their active patients had paused or canceled care. Several furloughed staff members never returned.

The most difficult shift was cultural. Riverside's leadership had to confront a hard truth: just because a system is external doesn't mean the risk is. The breach didn't come through their front door—but they paid the price all the same.

Lessons Learned: A Breach Doesn't Need to Start with You to Hurt You

- Third-party disruptions can have the same impact as internal failures.
- Redundant billing workflows, even partial ones, can keep cash flow moving.
- Communication plans for patients during downtime preserve trust.
- Vendor contracts should include breach notification and response obligations.
- Crisis response teams must be empowered to act even without full clarity.

Key Takeaways for Executives

- Conduct a vendor risk audit and identify your most critical dependencies.
- Establish manual fallback procedures for billing, claims, and eligibility checks.

- Train staff on how to talk about data privacy during third-party disruptions.
- Require vendor contracts to include breach clauses and continuity guarantees.
- Don't wait for a crisis to test your response—practice it now.

Final Thoughts: What You Don't Control Still Impacts You

Riverside Family Clinic survived, but the breach exposed cracks in their systems, assumptions, and leadership readiness.

They learned that resilience isn't about avoiding disruption; it's about preparing for it. Even when the problem begins outside your organization, the impact lands on your desk.

As an executive, your job isn't just to protect what you manage directly. It's to anticipate the risks of what you rely on. In healthcare, delay equals disruption. And disruption costs trust, care, and continuity.

"It takes as much energy to wish as it does to plan."

—Eleanor Roosevelt

CHAPTER 8

Trial by Fire

"The time to repair the roof is when the sun is shining."
—John F. Kennedy

Wildfires are nothing new in California. Every year, residents brace themselves for fire season, hoping that this time, their homes, businesses, and communities will be spared.

But in 2025, the firestorm that engulfed parts of Los Angeles and Ventura counties exceeded anything most communities had prepared for. Fueled by high winds, extreme drought, and bone-dry vegetation, the fires exploded with terrifying speed.

This is a story about more than flames. It's a story about two counties, two businesses, and two very different outcomes. It's about what happens when you plan for the worst. For others, it was a grim reminder of the devastating consequences of being unprepared.

The Firestorm Ignites

It began on January 14, 2025, with a small brush fire in the hills outside Ojai, a quiet town in Ventura County. What started as a minor incident grew into a monstrous blaze within hours, driven by Santa Ana winds gusting over 60 miles per hour. Embers leapt miles ahead of the fire line, sparking spot fires in Los Angeles County and forcing tens of thousands to evacuate.

Ventura's emergency response teams acted swiftly. Alerts were sent out across multiple platforms, SMS, automated calls, even social media posts. Fire crews had already been deployed to high-risk zones. Local shelters opened immediately, staffed by volunteers trained in wildfire response protocols.

Meanwhile, several Los Angeles County communities found themselves caught off guard. Outdated emergency communication systems delayed evacuation notices. Some neighborhoods received no warning until the flames were already visible. With evacuation routes clogged and no clear guidance, many families faced chaos and confusion as they tried to flee.

Two Businesses, Two Realities

The fire didn't discriminate, but the outcomes did. Two local businesses, similar in size, industry, and location, faced the same threat. Their preparation made all the difference.

Mendoza & Co. Accounting: A Model of Preparedness

Maria Mendoza, owner of a 19-person CPA firm in Ventura County, had seen this before. After the devastating 2017 Thomas Fire, she overhauled her business continuity strategy. She wasn't going to be caught off guard again.

Here's how Mendoza & Co. stayed operational:

- **Cloud-Based Systems:** Every client record, tax file, and communication thread was stored securely in encrypted cloud-based platforms. There were no paper files to lose.

- **Remote Work Protocols:** Staff had laptops, secure communication setup, and designated check-in procedures. When the fire hit, they simply relocated. Many worked from hotels, friends' homes, or temporary shelters.

- **Prewritten Client Communications:** Automated messages let clients know services continued without interruption. Outreach was immediate, transparent, and reassuring.

While the fire was terrifying, they had a plan and executed it. Despite three weeks of forced office closure, Mendoza & Co. didn't lose a single client or miss a single tax deadline.

Walters, Langley & Pierce LLP: A Costly Oversight

Thirty miles away in Los Angeles County, the story at Walters, Langley & Pierce LLP unfolded very differently. The 55-person law firm specialized in complex litigation and corporate counsel, yet they had never completed a formal disaster recovery plan. Their continuity strategy amounted to hoping for the best.

When the evacuation order came, chaos followed:

- **No Central Leadership:** With no plan, no one knew who should coordinate the firm's response.

- **Limited Remote Access:** Most case files were on local servers. A few attorneys had limited access via laptop, but with power down in many areas, access was sporadic.

- **No Cloud System:** Without digital filing tools, even those working remotely couldn't retrieve documents, meet deadlines, or communicate with courts and clients effectively.

One small grace was that the courts shut down, too, buying the firm a few days of breathing room. But even that wasn't enough. Missed filings, dropped communication threads, and unanswered client inquiries began stacking up.

Several of the firm's largest clients quietly transitioned to other firms. When the smoke cleared, the loss was visible, not just in revenue, but in relationships, reputation, and team morale.

CHAPTER 9

Locked In

"The great thing about automation is that it works. The scary thing about automation is that it works."

—Anonymous

Natural disasters are expected. Businesses plan for hurricanes, earthquakes and floods. But the threat that nearly turned deadly for Atlantic Distribution Services wasn't a storm; it was technology.

In the summer of 2024, a cyberattack targeting vulnerable IoT (Internet of Things) devices triggered a massive power outage that swept across parts of the Eastern Seaboard. Millions were affected. Among them was a mid-sized distribution center in Norfolk, Virginia, where employees found themselves trapped inside a building they couldn't escape.

This is the story of how a state-of-the-art system became a liability, and how assumptions about technology nearly turned a blackout into a tragedy.

The Cyberattack That Sparked the Blackout

On July 18, 2024, cybercriminals launched a coordinated attack exploiting flaws in high-wattage IoT devices including smart thermostats, connected appliances, and HVAC controls, remotely triggering sudden fluctuations in power demand. The chaos cascaded through the grid; substations failed, power systems overloaded, and within 15 minutes, the region was plunged into darkness.

At Atlantic Distribution Services, 18 employees were starting a regular shift. The lights blinked off. Machines stopped humming. At first, they assumed it was temporary. Then, the digital locks failed.

The building's high-tech security system, controlled by a cloud-connected access platform, defaulted to full lockdown. Employees in the breakroom and warehouse found themselves sealed in with no way out.

When Safety Becomes a Trap

The attack had taken out power and communications. There were no phones and no internet, no ways to call for help. Their backup generator, installed several months earlier, didn't start. It had never been tested and the fuel had never been rotated.

Inside the windowless warehouse, the temperature climbed quickly. With no air circulation, the heat became stifling. Thousands of lithium-ion batteries, awaiting shipment, began to pose a safety risk. In high heat, they become volatile.

Panic began to set in.

Attempts to override the security system failed, as the manual bypass required an internet connection to authenticate, a critical design flaw. Reinforced windows couldn't be opened. Steel emergency doors wouldn't disengage.

A Terrifying Two Hours

It wasn't until nearly two hours later that a family member of a missing employee called 911. First responders arrived quickly, but with no working override codes, they too were locked out.

Firefighters eventually used hydraulic tools to force open a loading dock door. Employees, dehydrated and overheated, were led out. Several required medical attention for heat exhaustion. Fortunately, no one was critically injured.

But the risk had been real.

Power Returns, But Recovery Falters

Electricity was restored the following day. But for Atlantic Distribution, the real crisis was only beginning.

The security system failed to reboot. Some doors remained locked. Others were stuck open. The IoT-connected surveillance system still needed remote authentication, but internet service hadn't returned.

Conveyor belts, robotic sorters, and scanners had to be manually recalibrated. Several on-premise servers were corrupted by the abrupt shutdown. Worse, the IT team had never rehearsed a full recovery scenario.

Entire sections of the facility were unusable. Shipments missed deadlines. Client relationships suffered. Employee morale cratered.

Losses totaled in the millions. Major contracts were renegotiated, and some were lost entirely. Several staff members quit in the weeks that followed. Most painfully of all, trust—both internally and with clients—had been deeply shaken.

Lessons Learned: The Technology Trap

- Critical systems were configured to *fail secure*—locking doors—instead of *fail safe* for emergency egress.
- Manual overrides depended on cloud-based authentication—an indefensible design in a power or internet outage.
- Backup power systems had never been tested under live conditions.
- Staff were untrained in full facility failure scenarios.
- There was no offline communication plan or fallback protocol for critical infrastructure.

Key Takeaways for Executives

- Manual overrides must be accessible without internet access.

- Backup systems should be tested quarterly—under live load.
- Fail-safe settings should prioritize life and safety.
- Your crisis playbook must include loss of power, connectivity, and internal communication.
- Redundancy must exist in both infrastructure and personnel.

Final Thoughts: When Innovation Becomes Liability

Atlantic Distribution survived, but barely. Their experience serves as a powerful warning for any organization chasing efficiency without preparing for failure.

Technology should empower, not endanger. Smart systems improve speed and precision, but without thoughtful risk planning, they become single points of failure.

Preparedness is not overreaction. It's the acknowledgment that not everything can be controlled.

When a crisis hits, the companies that ask tough questions ahead of time are the ones that survive. Because when Plan B fails, what's left is leadership, clarity, and the infrastructure you built when everything was still working.

"Trust, but verify."

—Ronald Reagan

CHAPTER 10

The Silent Heist—A Business Email Compromise Unveiled

"The greatest trick the devil ever pulled was convincing the world he didn't exist."

—Charles Baudelaire

Some breaches make headlines. Others slip quietly beneath the radar until the damage is already done.

For Harper & Reed, a well-established corporate law firm, trust was everything. Unfortunately, they found out too late that their biggest threat wasn't a massive cyberattack, but a single compromised email account.

Their reputation had been built over three decades of serving high-net-worth clients and Fortune 1000 companies, handling complex mergers, acquisitions, and litigation.

But in the spring of 2024, their trust in their own systems was shattered.

A single compromised email led to a financial loss of nearly half a million dollars, put their most valuable clients at risk, and exposed glaring weaknesses in their internal processes and communication.

This is the story of how a sophisticated Business Email Compromise (BEC) attack, combined with slow internal response, turned into a full-scale financial disaster.

The Unseen Intrusion

It began subtly. There was no ransomware note or system crash. Just a quiet login from a foreign IP address that was flagged, then ignored, in the company's email logs. The attacker created a forwarding rule that sent a blind copy of every email from the Senior manager's inbox to an external address.

For weeks, the attacker studied communication patterns. They learned the firm's tone, project timelines, invoicing structure, and client relationships. Eventually, they crafted a near-perfect fake invoice and sent it to a client from a spoofed domain that was just one character off from the real one. The message referenced a real project, matched the invoice format, and even copied the project manager's usual sign-off.

The email, routine as any other, contained detailed payment instructions that the attackers promptly intercepted. In a swift and calculated move, they altered the details—redirecting the funds to an offshore account they controlled.

The client paid the invoice. Nearly $170,000 was wired to the attacker's account.

It wasn't discovered until weeks later during routine financial reconciliation, and the client was irate. Harper & Reed had no idea the fraud had occurred. Their client had been the one defrauded, but the loss of trust affected both sides.

Fallout and Forensics

An internal audit revealed that the compromised email account also included multiple threads with embedded credentials, vendor access details, and internal discussions around contract negotiations.

The attackers hadn't just stolen money. They had accessed sensitive data that could be used for future scams or competitive intelligence. It was a silent heist with no ransom and no defacement, just cold and quiet theft.

Legal teams got involved. Clients were notified. Insurance claims were filed. Staff underwent emergency phishing training. Two key clients paused new contracts, citing concerns over data handling.

A Difficult but Necessary Reset

Harper & Reed brought in external cybersecurity advisors to audit their systems. Multifactor authentication was enforced across all cloud apps. Email filtering was tightened. External forwarding was disabled. Threat detection and response tools were added. Most importantly, they began to treat cybersecurity not as a technical problem, but as a business risk that required executive involvement.

The firm also implemented a clean inbox policy. No passwords in emails, no shared credentials, and quarterly inbox reviews to purge sensitive data.

Lessons Learned: The Quiet Ones Are the Most Dangerous

- Email compromises may not trigger alarms, but they can cause major damage.
- Attackers are patient and observant. Small gaps become big opportunities.
- Spoofed domains are easy to overlook, especially in fast-moving client conversations.
- Trust is easier to lose than recover.
- Cyber risk is not just an IT issue. It is a leadership issue.

Key Takeaways for Executives

- Assume attackers are watching. Build detection and response, not just prevention.
- Audit email security settings regularly, including forwarding rules and MFA status.
- Train staff to spot subtle red flags in emails, not just obvious scams.
- Review client communication protocols. Add second-step verification for high-dollar transactions.

- Integrate cybersecurity discussions into leadership meetings, not just IT updates.

Final Thoughts: When Silence Is the Threat

Harper & Reed didn't lose everything, but the breach changed their mindset.

Some threats make noise. Others wait in the quiet, exploiting routine and complacency. In a connected world, your weakest link is often your most trusted tool.

When trust is betrayed quietly, recovery requires more than tech. It requires rebuilding confidence from the inside out. As cyber threats continue to evolve, the question every executive must ask is simple: Are we doing everything we can to protect our organization before disaster strikes?

"The weakest link in the security chain is the human element."

—Kevin Mitnick

CHAPTER 11

The CEO's Secret—When One Person Holds All the Keys

"The graveyards are full of indispensable men."
—Charles de Gaulle

At Aegis AI, a fast-growing artificial intelligence startup known for its cutting-edge threat detection tools, the pace was relentless and the expectations were high. With a lean team, tight deadlines, and major enterprise clients to serve, the company was firing on all cylinders.

But beneath its polished exterior, a hidden vulnerability was growing, one that no firewall could stop.

The company's founder and CEO, Mira Sandoval, was a brilliant technologist. Visionary, driven, and fiercely protective of her creation, Mira had her fingerprints on every major system. She managed the AWS infrastructure, oversaw user provisioning, handled third-party integrations, and even maintained admin access to source code repositories. Mira was not just the founder;

she was the system administrator, dev ops lead, and unofficial incident response commander all in one.

Most tech executives surrounded themselves with robust leadership teams. Mira believed that too many cooks in the kitchen led to leaks, inefficiencies, and indecision. She trusted few people and, despite engaging a Board of Advisors, rarely shared key details about the company's financials, roadmap, or contingency plans.

The culture at Aegis AI celebrated this hands-on approach. Mira's deep involvement was seen as a strength, not a risk. That changed when she vanished.

When the Center Collapses

Mira embarked on a trip to Tokyo to finalize a major AI partnership. As usual, she traveled alone, taking only her personal laptop and phone, both containing the only copies of critical company documents.

But she never made it to the meeting.

While traveling, she developed severe respiratory complications and was rushed to the ICU in Tokyo. Unconscious and on life support, Mira was unable to communicate with anyone.

Back at Aegis AI's headquarters, panic set in. The Board of Advisors had no access to financial projections or investor commitments. The leadership team had no business continuity plan because Mira had never shared it. The product development team didn't know the full AI roadmap since Mira kept everything on her laptop. IT had no access to her personal devices, which contained everything necessary to keep the business running.

She had not designated a formal second-in-command with full technical access. The leadership team was left scrambling.

The engineering leads quickly discovered they could not push code updates. The production environment was locked behind multi-factor authentication tied to Mira's personal device. Several critical encryption keys were stored in her password manager. Billing details for multiple vendors were under her sole account. Even the internal wiki, used to document the infrastructure, required admin credentials that only she knew.

For a company that prided itself on cybersecurity, it had become completely exposed by its own overcentralization.

BYOD Culture—No Oversight, No Control

Mira's approach to secrecy extended beyond her own practices. She allowed her senior leadership and early employees to work from personal devices, creating a fragmented IT environment. Unlike the rest of the company, which was issued managed laptops with security protocols, the early employees, including Mira herself, used their own laptops, tablets, and phones.

This meant there were no centralized backups, no monitoring, and no IT oversight on these devices. If a laptop was lost, there was no way to recover data. If malware infected a device, there was no security policy to mitigate the risk.

When Aegis AI's Board of Advisors raised concerns, Mira dismissed them.

Scrambling for Access

The CTO and COO worked frantically to reset accounts, engage cloud providers, and regain access. Legal counsel initiated emergency actions to obtain access to company-owned digital assets. Vendors were cooperative, to a point, but the process was slow. Every hour of downtime meant missed client deliverables and mounting internal chaos.

Developers were blocked. Client reports were delayed. Payment processing systems were inaccessible. One client threatened to terminate their contract unless service was restored within 48 hours.

The realization set in quickly. Mira's brilliance had become a single point of failure.

Recovery and Rebuilding

With help from external advisors, Aegis AI slowly regained control. The team established an incident response plan specifically for executive incapacitation. Passwords were moved into a shared vault with appropriate permissions. Admin rights were redistributed. Systems were audited for privilege escalation vulnerabilities.

A succession plan was formalized. Documentation became a requirement, not an afterthought. Every new employee now received onboarding that included business continuity training. The cultural shift was significant: from heroic centralization to resilient delegation.

Mira eventually returned, and to her credit, fully supported the changes. She admitted that while she built Aegis with security in mind, she had overlooked the security risks that come from human dependencies.

Lessons Learned: Even the Smartest Systems Fail Without People Plans

- Overcentralized leadership can paralyze operations.
- Admin rights must be shared across roles and documented. Succession and incapacity plans are critical at every level.
- Password managers are only helpful when others can access them appropriately.
- Executive absence is a business continuity scenario, not just an HR issue.

Key Takeaways for Executives

- Conduct a human dependency audit across all systems and workflows.
- Distribute access credentials with appropriate oversight and policy.
- Prepare for executive incapacity just as you would for technical outages.

- Build a culture where knowledge is shared and risks are acknowledged.
- Ensure IT, legal, and HR collaborate on continuity protocols.

Final Thoughts: Resilience Means Redundancy, Including Leadership

Aegis AI didn't get hacked, breached, or flooded. What nearly broke them was a founder in a hospital bed with no backup. Every business has critical systems. When those systems live in one person's head, they become liabilities, not assets.

If your CEO disappears tomorrow, can your company still operate? If the answer is no, then you don't have a business continuity plan. You have a single point of failure.

Build the team. Share but protect the keys, because when Plan B fails, your people, not just your systems, must be ready.

"If you want to go fast, go alone. If you want to go far, go together."
—African Proverb

CHAPTER 12

The Unseen Heist—When Growth Outpaces Security

"Growth is never by mere chance; it is the result of forces working together."

—James Cash Penney

Vector Precision, a small but rapidly expanding engineering consultancy, had built a reputation for high-precision mechanical and structural design. Founded by a close-knit group of engineers, the firm had grown into a global operation with employees spread across multiple countries. Frequent travel to client sites, on-the-ground inspections, and collaborative engineering plans became routine.

Despite their technical success, the founders focused almost exclusively on engineering output while largely ignoring operational security. As engineers, they assumed their data wasn't of much value outside their own niche. Who would even want this data? *It's only useful for our specific projects*, they believed.

With no dedicated IT or cybersecurity staff, those responsibilities fell to Jason Kemp, a senior engineer who managed tech support alongside his full-time engineering workload. This patchwork approach resulted in several blind spots:

- No data classification policy, making it difficult to distinguish between sensitive and non-sensitive files.
- No tools to detect or prevent unauthorized data transfers.
- Personal devices used freely, including for capturing proprietary images on job sites. Despite a policy requiring centralized file storage, most employees saved work locally.
- No monitoring in place to flag unusual access patterns or downloads.

A Growing Company, A Fracturing Culture

Jason voiced concerns about these risks, but his warnings were dismissed. Leadership viewed security protocols as distractions from productivity.

As the firm expanded beyond 100 employees, its culture began to fracture. The early camaraderie faded, and turnover increased. To meet demand, Vector Precision subcontracted more work to outside firms and freelancers, offering them the same data access as internal staff. Trust began to feel like an outdated notion.

Then came the breach, only it wasn't external. It came from within.

Four senior engineers, each leading different departments, secretly coordinated their departure from Vector Precision to launch a competing firm. Over the course of two months, they downloaded key project files, pricing templates, client contact lists, and engineering models. They also used their company email accounts to subtly inform clients about their new venture.

When the four engineers resigned simultaneously on a Friday afternoon, the leadership team was blindsided. By Monday, the four had launched a new engineering firm. Somehow, they had already secured contracts with several of Vector's top clients.

Without monitoring systems in place, the theft had gone entirely unnoticed. By the time legal action began, it was too late. The damage had already been done.

Rebuilding in the Wake of an Internal Breach

The fallout was devastating. Major clients defected. Morale plummeted. Internal trust evaporated. Legal costs mounted into the hundreds of thousands as the company tried to prove theft of intellectual property.

One employee summed up the collective feeling: "If four of our top engineers saw a reason to leave and take our clients with them, what does that say about the rest of us?"

Vector Precision eventually rebuilt, but the incident left lasting scars. Leadership implemented stronger data classification rules, onboarded a full-time IT manager, and installed data loss prevention and monitoring tools. All employees were required to use secure, company-managed devices. They also revisited every contractor agreement to include stricter data handling clauses.

More importantly, they started investing in their culture again—offering clearer career paths, team-building efforts, and channels for internal concerns.

Lessons Learned: When Growth Outpaces Controls

- Data that seems specialized can still be weaponized by insiders.
- Assigning IT responsibilities to engineers is not a scalable or secure solution.
- Monitoring tools must be in place before they are needed, not after the damage is done.
- Company loyalty isn't permanent. It must be cultivated and protected.
- Protecting intellectual property requires proactive controls, not just legal reactions.

Key Takeaways for Executives

- Conduct human risk audits to identify access-related vulnerabilities.
- Enforce data classification and device management for all personnel.
- Build a layered security program with monitoring and incident response tools.

- Update onboarding and offboarding policies to reflect real risk.
- Treat internal culture as a strategic asset—it may be your first line of defense.

Final Thoughts: Betrayal is a Risk You Can Plan For

Vector Precision wasn't hacked by an outsider. It was wounded from within. The very people trusted to build the business used their access to tear it apart.

In today's data-driven world, the biggest threats may not come from anonymous hackers—they may come from inside your own network, carrying out the "perfect crime" using tools *you* gave them.

Build safeguards. Build culture. And above all, never assume your team would never do what others already have.

"Security is not a product, but a process."

—Bruce Schneier

CHAPTER 13

The Playbook for Survival— Lessons from the Edge of Disaster

"You can't wait for the storm to start building the levee."
—Anonymous

If there's one lesson this book reinforces, it's this: crisis never arrives at a convenient time. When disruption strikes, whether from a ransomware attack, supply chain collapse, leadership vacuum, or natural disaster, only the prepared endure.

We've seen law firms blindsided by business email compromise. Manufacturers brought to a halt by chip shortages and facility fires. Healthcare clinics crippled by third-party vendor outages. Executives paralyzed by over-centralized control. Each of these stories revealed the same truth. These organizations believed they had a backup plan. But when that plan failed, so did their confidence.

This chapter brings it all together. The stories you've read point to a foundational truth. Business resilience is no longer optional. It is the difference between bouncing back and breaking apart.

It starts with:

People

Who steps in when a leader is unavailable? Do teams understand their roles during a crisis?

It is not enough to protect systems. You must protect continuity in decision-making.

Process

Are your workflows clearly documented, routinely tested, and flexible enough to adapt under pressure?

A strong process defines not only what must be done but how and by whom, even when systems are down.

Technology

Can your business function without internet access, a cloud provider, or your primary software platform?

Every operation should have secure backups, offline capabilities, and manual alternatives built in.

What We've Learned

Let's revisit a few of the hard-earned insights shared throughout this book:

- From Northpoint Manufacturing (Chapter 4): Cutting IT budgets may save money in the short term, but it can cost everything when recovery efforts fall short.
- From Greenfield Motors (Chapter 5): Outsourcing does not remove risk. When your vendor fails, your business pays the price.
- From Harper and Reed (Chapter 9): A single overlooked email led to a six-figure loss. Without proper training and controls, trust becomes a vulnerability.
- From Aegis AI (Chapter 10): When one person controls all the access and decision points, your continuity plan is already compromised.
- From Atlantic Distribution (Chapter 8): A smart building became a trap when no one had considered what would happen if power and connectivity were lost.

From Insights to Action

Real resilience begins by asking difficult but essential questions:

- What happens if the CEO cannot be reached?
- What if our software provider disappears tomorrow?
- What if we lose access to our building or our cloud systems?
- What if our backups are corrupted or incomplete?

These are not just theoretical questions. These are real-world scenarios that companies have faced. The only difference between survival and collapse was preparation.

Ready to Build Your Own Playbook?

If these stories resonated with you, take the next step:

Access Our Tools:

We have created practical resources to help your business move forward, including:

- A step-by-step business continuity guide
- An interactive Excel workbook for collecting and managing continuity data
- A preparation checklist that aligns your people, processes, and technology

https://planb.bizcomglobal.com/

Final Thoughts: The Cost of Inaction

Crisis does not care how successful you were yesterday. You will not rise to the level of your goals. You will fall to the level of your readiness.

Whether you lead a growing small business or a large enterprise, the path forward is the same.

Understand your risks. Build your plans. Prepare your people. Test every system.

Because when Plan B fails, the only ones who continue leading are the ones who were ready.

"Expect the best, plan for the worst, and prepare to be surprised."
—Denis Waitley

CHAPTER 14

When You're Ready to Act

"You don't rise to the occasion—you fall to the level of your preparation."

—Archilochus

You've just finished reading real-world stories of disruption—from companies locked out of their systems to organizations blindsided by third-party failures and leadership missteps. These weren't hypothetical case studies. They were preventable disasters. And the difference between those who survived and those who didn't came down to one thing:

Preparation.

Now, it's your turn.

The BizCom Global 5 Pillar Risk Assessment

If you're unsure where to start, begin here.

The 5 Pillar Business & Technology Risk Assessment is a complimentary tool developed by BizCom Global to help executives evaluate their business preparedness across five critical dimensions:

- Managed IT – Are your systems supported, updated, and aligned to how your business operates?
- Cybersecurity – Are your controls configured for prevention, detection, and response to real-world threats?
- Compliance – Can you meet the regulatory or contractual obligations tied to your industry? What about audit readiness?
- IT Ecosystem – Are your tools and integrations cohesive, or is technical debt slowing you down and increasing risk?
- Business Continuity – If something fails, do you know how to respond, how fast you can recover, and who's responsible?

This isn't just an IT scan. It's a business-aligned assessment that evaluates how your people, processes, and technologies work together to support both resilience and productivity.

You'll receive:

- A readiness score across each pillar
- Insight into your blind spots
- Strategic guidance to strengthen your foundation
- Start your free assessment at https://planb.bizcomglobal.com/

Have a Conversation

If you want to talk through your specific situation, I invite you to book a confidential 1-on-1 conversation directly with me. Whether you're navigating uncertainty, building a plan from scratch, or wondering what's next—let's talk.

Schedule your call at https://planb.bizcomglobal.com/

Final Thoughts

Resilience isn't a switch you flip in an emergency. It's a discipline you build every day.

This book has shown what happens when organizations plan ahead—and what happens when they don't. Now the choice is yours.

You've seen what can go wrong. You've seen what others did to recover. Now it's time to take action before it's your company in the headlines.

Let's make sure your Plan B doesn't fail, because the future belongs to the prepared.

"In the middle of every difficulty lies opportunity."

—Albert Einstein

ABOUT THE AUTHOR

Mark Wiener is the founder and CEO of BizCom Global, a firm specializing in business continuity, cybersecurity, compliance, strategic IT leadership, and providing Managed IT services to SMBs. Over the past two decades, he has helped businesses navigate moments of crisis they never anticipated from cyberattacks and regulatory pitfalls to natural disasters and internal breakdowns. His approach blends technology with practical business sense, earning him a reputation as a trusted advisor to organizations across a wide range of industries.

His early experiences working in both the corporate world and as a volunteer taught him the importance of thinking clearly under pressure, allocating limited resources, and making life-altering decisions in real time. These are the same principles he brings into the boardrooms and planning sessions of companies preparing for the worst and striving to come out stronger.

Outside of his professional life, Mark is deeply committed to his community. He has served as a volunteer and board member for numerous local nonprofit organizations, chambers of commerce, and service committees. His passion for public service and organizational resilience often intersect, shaping his belief that strong leadership and practical preparedness can save businesses, just as it can save lives.

When he's not helping companies plan for the unexpected, you'll find Mark mentoring emerging leaders, speaking at national conferences, or swapping war stories with fellow business owners about the day everything went sideways and what they did next.